I Am In Pieces

Christian Blue

BookLeaf Publishing

India | USA | UK

Presentation by *BookLeaf Publishing*

Web: www.bookleafpub.com

E-mail: info@bookleafpub.com

ISBN: 9789358315110

First edition 2023

*I dedicate this book to everyone who has taken
the time to read my poetry, even just a line of it.
From those who scrolled past on social media
to those who turned the pages of my earliest
notebooks, this is for you.*

*Most of all, I dedicate this book to you, reader.
This is for you, and my only hope is that it
moves something within you, changes your life
in a positive way, however small.*

ACKNOWLEDGEMENT

I would like to thank everyone who has helped me get this far in my writing. Thank you to all the teachers I've had from elementary all through college that encouraged and challenged me to write, especially those that allowed me to practice my creative works. Thank you to the friends and family who supported me, and thank you to everyone who inspired great feelings in me, good or bad. Without you, I would not have anything to write about.

PREFACE

Hello, everyone, and thank you for picking up my book. I wrote this while thinking on some of the hardest times in my life and how I ended up where I am today. I have endured great darkness, and it follows me even as I have built a life I am quite content with. These poems are about my struggle coming to terms with the darkness and learning to let light in beside it. I wrote this thinking of everyone out there who may be like me, who is hurting with no end in sight. You are not alone, and you are not broken. You are loved, and I have poured all of my heart into these poems to show it.

I Must Admit

I have lost myself,
I have lost my voice,
I have forgotten the words, yet
I still have this longing for you
        to hear me,
        to tell you something.

I always said I would shout it
        at the top of my lungs,
        if ever given the chance, and
I now have that chance, but I fear
it is too late,
it is all gone, the person I used to be.

I must find myself again,
I must break my voice out of my throat
        and fling it to the wind,
        to find you, the one
I am still searching
for, a friend, it is all I ever wanted.

I believe it is all anyone wants, a friend,
        someone who sees you, hears you, and
smiles,

       someone who knows you and wants you
only
         to be yourself
    someone who is there, no matter what
    someone who you love so clearly
      they never call it into question
    someone like you, or so I'd like to
assume,
most would make the best of friends,
    if ever we took the chance.

I would like to take the chance with you,
    if even just through this ink and page.

I'm writing poetry within poetry
    simply to say,
I love you, to those who need to hear it as
I needed to hear it, for so long so
I will not make another person wait another
moment.

You are loved so dearly, being yourself is
enough.

we need both

am I a philosopher
or an artist,
trying to make sense of the world
or discover a new one,
am I searching for beauty
or creating it

my mind and my heart
always at war and yet,
always reaching for the same thing
if only they could work together once,
see wanting peace and wanting happiness
only make sense when together

who am I
when always so torn,
must I choose
or suffer the loss of both,
if you tear something in two is
it simply not half of what it once was?

how does one unravel a universe

I want to be myself with you,
let you into my mind
but I don't know where to start
my whole life

I don't know what's important
or if you'd even want to hear
all I know is
all I crave is someone near

come so close you can see me
truly hear me, please
I am so much more than I seem
you will find a universe underneath

how does one unravel a universe?
how does one shrink a universe
        to a single conversation?
how does one truly trust enough
        to open their universe to another?
I may never know the answer to these questions

all I know is you,
you too are a universe,

and each of us is bursting with life,
and I'd love to get to know yours, but

would you like to spend time in mine?

deeper

I think I should dive deeper
into something that makes us the same,
the feeling of pain,
I've swam in oceans of it
I just wish people knew
even those who can swim can drown

the water became my friend,
the only one that understood
the water became my home,
the only one that was always there
I became like the water,
cold but strong

after 20 years, the tides finally lowered
but I was afraid of dry land
and I called out for the storm over and over
Don't leave me alone,
I know nothing of this place,
I do not belong here!

of course, there is no truly escaping the water—
the world is made of it,
we are all made of it
but as the waves crashed over me again

I found myself numb, I had changed
but I remembered my friend, my home

from then, the ocean formed a cloud above me
and followed everywhere I went
and now, people avoid my rain, longing to be
dry
but I see theirs and invite it closer,
unafraid and knowing
the loneliness is worse than the water's touch

in the twilight

I was told time would bring peace,
and time brought her

it's true, I've known love before
but never like this, like her soul
fits perfectly beside mine,
so different and yet the same
right where it matters

she's always felt safest in the dark,
and I've always chased the light
now we sit together in the twilight,
her quietly enjoying the rays on her skin,
I no longer so afraid of the dark

we met with holes in both of our chests,
different shapes but we both know the feeling
of missing something

she grew thorns and I forged armor,
I was the first to embrace her, and
she as the first to embrace me tight

I wouldn't let her give up on love, and
she wouldn't let me give up on joy, and

we wouldn't let each other go, and
when the world spat at our grasped hands,
we held on tighter

she told me her secrets made everyone leave
I said to tell me them all and
watch me stay

I told her I'm in pieces
she took them in both her hands
and said she loved them all

fragmented

black and white and blank,
this is what it feels like to
dissociate.

it's buzzing, or is it fuzzy?
I don't know but it can't be
nothing.

just one word,
make it mean something, they need to know
you heard.

everything, it is just too much,
for one soul, one mind on pause or
just glitching.

this is what I mean,
I am broken, don't say I'm not
okay. I know I'm not.

reading this back
I just want to laugh, what sense does it make
to anyone else?

I find I cannot finish this,

I'm slipping like water, slips through fingers—
don't go yet.

nothing is worse

crying yourself to sleep
alone
just wanting them to hear
making sure they don't

knowing as a child
your parents' room
was not a safe place
to run after nightmares

it was a nightmare

eyes burning
chest caving in
that feeling echoing
through years of trauma
it is over now and yet
it happens over and over again
in my mind

I will never escape
those endless nights

even when I am no longer alone
in my bed

there is someone to listen

silent for so long
I have forgotten how to speak
hidden myself so well
I have lost myself

all of this pain
and all I can think
I'm so sorry

if it was never my fault
why is the weight of it all still
so heavy on
my shoulders?

missing

depression called me on the phone
asked what he always asks
how do I feel?
he always knows the answer

my soul is shattering
within me, the shards
seep the blood
I don't know how I still bleed

the depression asked
where are all my friends?
silence
then he laughed, he knew

I lost them long ago
the picture is so blurry I wonder
if they were ever there at all
the ones I loved, the ones
who were supposed to love me too

what do you want?
when I grew tired of the memories
depression sounded sad
didn't I miss him?

I feel it start to rain
but I am inside   15
I realize maybe I did
I see I am reaching out for his hand

GOD LOVES YOU

everything I am is exactly
       what I am meant to be
for I was created perfectly
       by a God who loves me
yes I am changing my body
       not that it was not beautiful
I was who I needed to be
when I needed to be
       to become who I truly am
a child of God only created to love
       (an action of which
one would never be judged)
now I know I needed to know both
       to become a bridge for all
God does not make mistakes
       but that does not mean
you are not meant to change
God does not put you at the finish line
       He puts you were you need to be
       to reach it in the end
all life endures pain and He knows
       it is essential but never easy
just know you are never alone
       no matter what they say
       you are loved

recklessly
perfectly
unconditionally
endlessly

        by the Creator of the universe
        whoever you believe that to be
I know you feel it somewhere inside
        that ability to love
        comes only from being loved

in between

there once was a boy
      who never fit in

too fast for those who walked
      not fast enough for those who ran
too mature for the young
      too young for the old
too social for the loners
      too lonely for the teams
too peaceful for the fighters
      too much of a fighter for the pacifists
too realistic for the believers
      too faithful for the skeptics
too passionate for the empty
      too empty for the full of life
too put together for the broken
      too broken for the whole

he was caught
in between it all
not out of neutrality
but out of passion for unity
      understanding and kindness

not accepted by either side

he got to see them both
from the outside
        they don't look so different

what's the purpose of life?

some people know
some people don't and
some people are okay with that—
I am not

I have been asking myself this
all my life and never found
an answer anywhere I looked—
I have looked everywhere

the answer must be Love
Love created the universe
Love saved me, so I loved—
I am still lost

Love stays with me though they left
I wonder if it's something I have done
or something I do not do—
I am sorry

I cannot look back or forward
all I see is dark with no way to know
if I am going the right direction—
I am trying (so hard)

no one can help
no one sees me, no one knows
I got this far on my own and realized—
I do not want to do it (alone) anymore

I am more than one part of me

it's not that I'm just sad
all the time, it's just
nothing else about me makes sense
without the sadness

I smile
       but it is through the pain
I love
       but it is in spite of the hate
       they have shown me
I see the bright side
       but only knowing the dark side
       is right beside it
I refuse to quit
       but it is while fully knowing
how hard it will be
I continue to fight
       but it is with a broken heart
       and a fractured soul

I don't want you to see
just a part of me unless
you will see all of me

it gets lonely sometimes knowing
half the population will never be able to
            understand me
and the other half will never even try
though I will spend the rest of my life trying
            to change that

afraid

when did I become
        so afraid

a new place
a new friend
all things new

going to the store
going outside at night
going outside at all

spiders
(it's always been spiders
but lately its been anything
        with legs)

letting you see my work
letting you see me

the future
the present
the past haunting me
        forever

feeling like this

forever

needing you
          again
you not being here
          again

telling you
you never knowing

getting it all wrong
never being enough
never getting better
always feeling this alone

waking up
being alive

to the old me

I don't know when it went
       from you to me
or if there was someone else
       in between
at some point I turned and
       you were back there
no longer in the mirror

there's so much I want
       to talk about
I wish you could see me
I wish you weren't vanishing
with every step I take
away from you

I've kept you close
       in my core
I'm trying to keep you
       happy
but I've lost what it means
       to you
       to me

I still know you
maybe better than I have ever
       known myself

I know you are waiting
for someone to come save you
for someone to love you
and actually treat you like it
for someone to say you are enough
for someone to show you the way
for life
to get better

so here it is
no one saves you
        you save yourself
no one loves you the way they should
        but God's love is the only love
        that is fulfilling
        and you will have that forever
no matter the fact that no one says it
        you are enough
no one will show you the way
        but you will find it yourself
life does not get better
        for a long time
        but it will

most importantly (know
I am crying now, too)
I'm proud of you
I love you
I miss you

motivated

how do you find motivation
when the time they said would heal
      hasn't
the people who said they would stay
      left
the ones who were supposed to help
      hurt you
the things that once brought enjoyment
      don't
the world, your only home is
      dying
people you don't even know
      control your rights
every little difference becomes a reason to
      judge and hate
the God you pray to has and always will be
      silent

when this happens, it's simple
when you can't find motivation
      create it
use your time to
      heal others
promise to stay and
      stay

don't hurt them
      help them
go out and find
      new enjoyment
don't keep killing the world
      rebuild it
don't let them take anything
      fight for your rights
face every difference with
      kindness and love
remember God acts, not speaks, and
      pray anyways

hair dye

I dyed my hair last night—
you know what that means

I was having a mental breakdown

are you okay?

a question I am never asked
but if I ever am
I lie, too panicked
to muster the courage
to tell the truth

as if they want to hear it

though it means no harm, the question
makes me angry
what am I supposed to say
when nothing is wrong
but no, I am not okay

has something happened today?

no, not today, but every single day of every
single year

from being a toddler to being a teenager
something did happen
many somethings were happening
over and over and over and—
it would probably hurt you to even hear it

so I keep my mouth shut,
hook the corners of my lips
into my colorless cheeks
and protect you from things
I needed protection from

yes I am okay
today, but I wasn't okay for so long
I can hardly see why it matters

honestly today my life is good
filled with a family I never had,
I built it with my own two hands
buried them both into the dirt
and grew this love from the ground of my soul

it is mine and
I will protect it with everything I have
from the people who hurt
and more importantly did not protect
me

so please just save your breath

I no longer care
if you care
if I am okay

homemade soup for the soul

I know you're sick
and I just wish
I could do something like
cook you homemade soup
then again what would that do
considering I can't cook
the only good I can do
here and now for you
is send something else
homemade

I'll write out the words with great care
like adding the secret ingredient to a meal
the ink flowing smoothly onto the paper
like fluffing your pillows
and filling you a glass of water
I'll tuck it into your pocket for you to keep close
like tucking you in with a warm blanket
and handing you your old stuffed animal
I'll choose only the sweetest words
reading them like the most gentle kisses
on your forehead and knuckles and cheek

I don't dot my I's but I'll cross every T
exactly as it should be

every part of the poem will be done perfectly
a beautiful piece of art
for your beautiful heart
so you can heal
and if we're being real
all that's bothering you
is a stomach flu
but I'll be real too
I'll take any excuse to write a poem for you

love is the answer

my world has always been
bleak, color beaten out of it
until all that was left was deep blues,
blacks and purples, but even then,
blues and purples got lonely, and faded to gray,
and black got scared, and faded, too.

I was colorblind and drowning in the fog,
but then a furious red cut through it all,
and I grasped onto it and I gasped into a world
of
pissed off, didn't begin to describe it.
misery and numbness had been condensed into
a black hole of rage and anger.

that blanket of red covered my world,
and that is how it stayed, until
you came along, and rather than trying to tear
the blanket that had become my shelter
off of my shoulders, you took the corners gently
and folded it into a beautiful rose.

Smile.

Stop.
That smile,
wear it more.
It is everything good.
It is the world falling into place.
It is hope for hope—
dreams becoming reachable again.
It is everything that is beautiful,
especially the way it reaches your eyes.
It is things that were never meant to be
separated
reunited.
It is ink for a blank page—
the creation of
something
from nothingness.
It is the embodiment of having a choice—
the creation of destiny.
It is faith
in whatever you believe—
the possibility of the impossible
(or, the not yet believed in).
It is finding joy
anywhere,
even in this world where everything is scarce.

It is simply everything,
in the form of one small thing.
It is everything love
was meant to be.

why I write

why do I write
    poetry
of all things, why is it
    something so many hate
    or will never understand
in a world of technology
    I picked up a pen
    and turned away from the screen
    just beginning to flicker to life
an outcast in so many ways
    I'm just trying
    to save the things
    that are dying
poetry is the perfect mix
    of words and art
    structured and abstract
    thoughtful and creative
poetry can capture anything
    emotion, the heart
    and the mind, somehow
    breaking words apart gives them more
meaning
I am not a typical poet
    I don't rhyme or count
    syllables, I can hardly spell

and I don't know all the rules
but I am a poet
	pouring my soul onto the page
	creating a bridge, connecting us all
	even if it only helps one person
because you are worth it
	all of you, even those who hate
	me, even those who hurt
	do not tell me otherwise
I will fight for you
	but I fight differently
	not bloodthirsty but
	love starved
I know the pain
	so I will show it and show you
	the light at the end of the tunnel
	is actually within you all along
I know you will not agree with everything I have
to say
	but I will say it anyways to tell you
	disagreements should not end
relationships
	there is middle ground, safe for us all
I do not want to lead you
	but I want to walk beside you
I will make mistakes
	like everyone else, that is okay
I will never give up
	on you, on us

on life, we can defeat death
again, this time it is on us

I suppose I write to
        speak to you all
    inspire you all
        fight for you all
        unite you all
        love you all

goodbye

is it always our fate
to say goodbye

I am haunted by the ones gone
too soon, by choice or not
I must be okay, smile
for they were in my life at all
and all I can do is the best I can
for the time our paths cross
and hope we both got all we needed
from each other in our lifetime

this is me doing my best
for you now, telling you everything
I can say, even if you can't hear it all
that's alright, I won't stop trying and
I will be back, with even more
I am not done here

keep holding on, you are seen and
never forgotten, you've got a friend
our souls are connected from across
any length in the universe

I suppose I am getting dramatic
but I've been where you are and
it is so much worse than dramatic
it is real, and you are hurting and
you were innocent before it all
I know this doesn't change anything but
I am so sorry
you did not deserve it, no matter what
you've done, you deserved to be loved

I know you need more
than this, a tangible friend,
actions over words, a hug,
the pain to stop, hope to return,
blatant and unconditional love—
I've said it again and again but again
I love you and you are enough and
you will make it through this
one day, you'll have all that you need
and more, even if all I have is ink and a pen
I will fight for you until we both have nothing
left
and I believe there is always something left

they say all things come
to an end
and yet every ending is

a beginning
so perhaps this is not
goodbye
but see you soon
on the other side

-Your Friend Blue